Pebble® Plus

Halloween Fun

Trick-or-Treat Safety

by Megan Cooley Peterson

Consulting editor: Gail Saunders-Smith, PhD

CAPSTONE PRESS

a capstone imprint

Pebble Plus is published by Capstone Press,
1710 Roe Crest Drive, North Mankato, Minnesota 56003
www.capstonepub.com

Library of Congress Cataloging-in-Publication Data
Peterson, Megan Cooley.
Trick-or-treat safety / by Megan Cooley Peterson.
pages cm.—(Pebble Plus. Halloween Fun)
Includes bibliographical references and index.
Summary: "Simple text and full-color photographs describe trick-or-treat safety at Halloween"—Provided by publisher.
ISBN 978-1-4765-2182-4 (library binding)
ISBN 978-1-4765-3493-0 (eBook PDF)
1. Halloween—Safety measures—Juvenile literature. I. Title.
GT4965.P42 2013
394.2646—dc23   2013006884

Editorial Credits
Jeni Wittrock, editor; Heidi Thompson, designer; Wanda Winch, media researcher; Jennifer Walker, production specialist

Photo Credits
Images by Capstone Studio: Karon Dubke, except: Dreamstime: Vitaliy Rozhkov, Halloween icons;
Shutterstock: olga.lolipops, border

Note to Parents and Teachers

The Halloween Fun set supports social studies standards related to holidays and culture. This book
describes and illustrates safe practices for trick-or-treating. The images support early readers in
understanding the text. The repetition of words and phrases helps early readers learn new words.
This book also introduces early readers to subject-specific vocabulary words, which are defined in
the Glossary section. Early readers may need assistance to read some words and to use the Table of
Contents, Glossary, Read More, Internet Sites, and Index sections of the book.

Printed in the United States of America in North Mankato, Minnesota.
032013   007223CGF13

Table of Contents

Tricks and Treats

It's Halloween night.

The air turns cool, and leaves

drop from the trees.

A bat swoops overhead.

Time for trick-or-treating!

Collecting candy is a fun way

to celebrate Halloween.

Staying safe as you

trick-or-treat can be

just as fun.

Costume Safety

Witches, ghosts, and zombies

prowl the streets on Halloween.

Before you join them, stick

reflective tape to your costume.

Make sure drivers can see you.

Watch out for things that go bump in the night. To see clearly, wear face paint instead of a mask. Check for allergies before applying face paint.

Aye, matey! Keep your swordfights safe by using a sword made of foam or cardboard. Wood or metal props can be dangerous.

Neighborhood Safety

Bring along an adult

as you roam

the neighborhood.

Never trick-or-treat

by yourself.

As you zip from house to house,

watch out for zooming cars.

Look both ways before

crossing the street.

Stay on the sidewalk.

Only ring the doorbell
if a house has its porch
light on. Stay away from
open flames. Never go in
a stranger's house.

Candy Safety

Before you dig into your pile

of candy, have an adult check it.

If a candy wrapper is open,

throw away that piece.

Never eat homemade treats.

Ghostly Candy Bucket

Want to spook your friends while trick-or-treating? Carry a ghostly candy bucket made from stuff around the house.

What You Need

empty ice cream bucket with handle
white construction paper
glue
scissors
black construction paper
paintbrush
glow-in-the-dark green acrylic paint
white crepe paper streamers

To Make

1 Cover the bucket with white construction paper and glue in place.

2 Cut out eyes and a mouth from the black construction paper. Glue to the front of the bucket.

3 Paint over the eyes and mouth with glow-in-the-dark paint. Let it dry.

4 Cut long pieces of white streamers. Make sure each piece is a different length. Glue streamers around the rim of the bucket. Be careful not to glue any streamers over the ghost's face.

Glossary

allergy—an extremely high sensitivity to something; an allergy causes an unpleasant reaction, such as sneezing or a rash

celebrate—to do something fun on a special day

dangerous—likely to cause harm or injury

prop—an item used by an actor or performer during a show; people also use props at Halloween

reflective—having the ablility to throw back light

roam—to wander

Read More

Aloian, Molly. *Halloween.* Celebrations in My World. New York: Crabtree Pub. Company, 2009.

Bozzo, Linda. *Kooky Halloween Jokes to Tickle Your Funny Bone.* Funnier Bone Jokes. Berkeley Heights, N.J.: Enslow Publishers, 2013.

Schuette, Sarah L. *Halloween Hunt: A Spot-It Challenge.* Spot It. Mankato, Minn.: Capstone Press, 2011.

Internet Sites

FactHound offers a safe, fun way to find Internet sites related to this book. All of the sites on FactHound have been researched by our staff.

Here's all you do:

Visit www.facthound.com

Type in this code: 9781476521824

Super-cool stuff!

Check out projects, games and lots more at
www.capstonekids.com

Index

Word Count: 199
Grade: 1
Early-Intervention Level: 16.